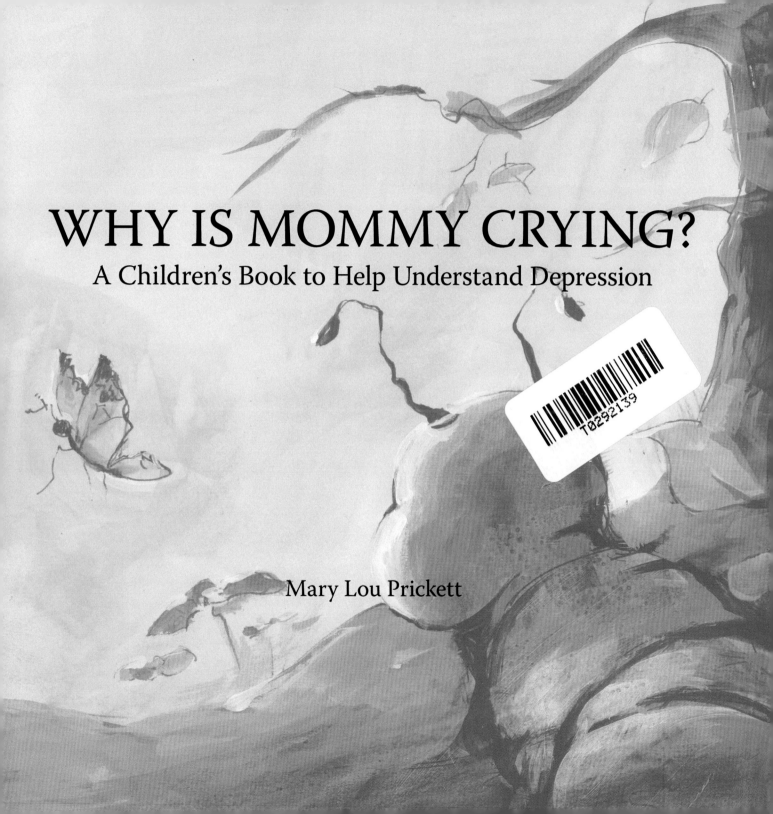

WHY IS MOMMY CRYING?

A Children's Book to Help Understand Depression

Mary Lou Prickett

AuthorHouse™
1663 Liberty Drive
Bloomington, IN 47403
www.authorhouse.com
Phone: 833-262-8899

This book is printed on acid-free paper.

ISBN: 978-1-4343-6472-2 (sc)
ISBN: 978-1-4685-9031-9 (e)

Library of Congress Control Number: 2008902242

Print information available on the last page.

Published by AuthorHouse 09/19/2022

authorHOUSE®

This book is dedicated to my sons, Robert and Christopher, who asked their own questions concerning my depression. Despite my illness, I am so proud of the fine, successful, happy, caring, Christian young men they have become. I LOVE YOU BOTH!

It was a bright and sunny springtime day.

All the little caterpillars were anxiously waiting for the time when they would become big beautiful butterflies.

The caterpillars were very happy, except for one…

Doobie.

Doobie watched as the butterfly moms flitted and
fluttered up and down, flower to flower….

except for Doobie's mom.

She usually hid by herself in the bushes and cried.

One day Doobie sat watching all the other caterpillars play. Suddenly, a pure white dove flew toward Doobie.

At first, Doobie was afraid!

"An angel of the Lord appeared…
but the angel said to them. "Do not be afraid!"

Luke 2:9

Soon the dove sat down beside Doobie.
She put her loving wing around him and he asked:

"Why is mommy crying? Have I done something wrong?
Is it my fault she cries? Is she mad at me? Does she love me?"

"Oh NO!...It is NOT your fault!" answered the dove.
"Your mommy loves you very much!
But, your mommy is sick with DEPRESSION.
She is just sad a lot of the time."

"Will she ever get better?" asked Doobie. "Oh YES!" replied the dove.

"She has doctors and medicine to help her!"....

...but, most of all, the Mighty Eagle loves her and wants to help her!"

Just then, Doobie's mom came out of the bush and began flying around in the bright sunlight.

Doobie was surprised to see the most beautiful, colorful, butterfly he had ever seen!

As Doobie's mom grew closer,
Doobie became a happy, little, colorful, butterfly too!

Doobie's mommy will always have her depression.
But, with the help of doctors and medicine, she will be
able to enjoy the beautiful flowers more often.

Most of all, it is Doobie's love and especially the love of the Mighty Eagle that will help her enjoy and love life again!

"...but those who hope in the Lord will renew their strength. They will soar on wings like eagles..."

Isaiah 40:31

THE END

Printed in the United States
by Baker & Taylor Publisher Services